JUL 19 1988
SEP 21 1988
MAR 9 1989
JUN 5 1989
AUG 1 0 1993
JAN 21 1993

JUVENILE

DULUTH PUBLIC LIBRARY
520 WEST SUPERIOR STREET
DULUTH, MINNESOTA 55802

‹ MACAO ›

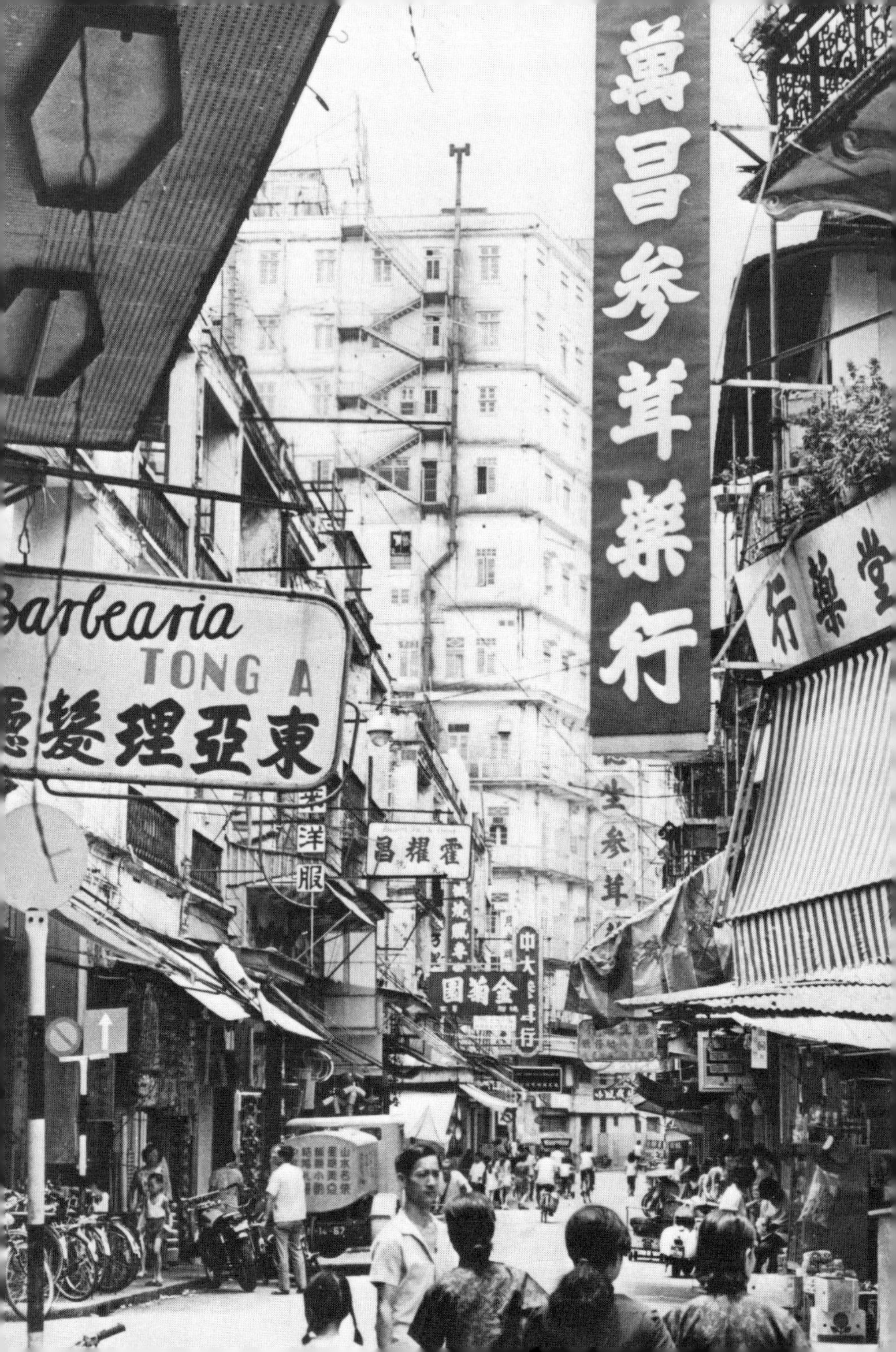

Barbearia
TONG A
東亞理髮
萬昌參茸藥行
堂藥行
洋服
霍耀昌
參茸
金菊園

PLACES AND PEOPLES OF THE WORLD
MACAO

T. Jeff Williams

CHELSEA HOUSE PUBLISHERS
New York • New Haven • Philadelphia

COVER: Although it belonged to Portugal for centuries, Macao has an Oriental culture. This park features a Chinese-style pavilion.

Editorial Director: Rebecca Stefoff
Editor: Rafaela Ellis
Copy Editor: Crystal G. Norris
Art Director: Janice Engelke
Designer: Maureen McCafferty
Photo Editor: Martin Baldessari
Photo Research: Patrick McCaffrey

Copyright © 1988 by Chelsea House Publishers,
a division of Main Line Book Co. All rights reserved.
Printed in the United States of America.

First Printing

1 3 5 7 9 8 6 4 2

Library of Congress Cataloging-in-Publication Data

Williams, T. Jeff.
Macao.
Includes index.
Summary: Surveys the history, topography, people, and culture of Macao, with emphasis on its current economy, industry, and place in the political world.
1. Macao. [1. Macao]
I. Title.
DS796.M2W55   1988   951'.26   87-18267
ISBN 1-55546-786-5

JUVENILE
915.126

◄CONTENTS►

Map 6
Facts at a Glance 9
History at a Glance 11
Chapter 1 Macao and the World 15
Chapter 2 A Coastal Outpost 21
Chapter 3 A History of Trade 25
Chapter 4 A Rich Culture 37
            Color Section Scenes of Macao 41
Chapter 5 Land of Contrasts 59
Chapter 6 Government and Social Services 67
Chapter 7 Revitalizing a Trade Economy 77
Chapter 8 A Last Look at Macao 85
Glossary 89
Index 93

CHINA

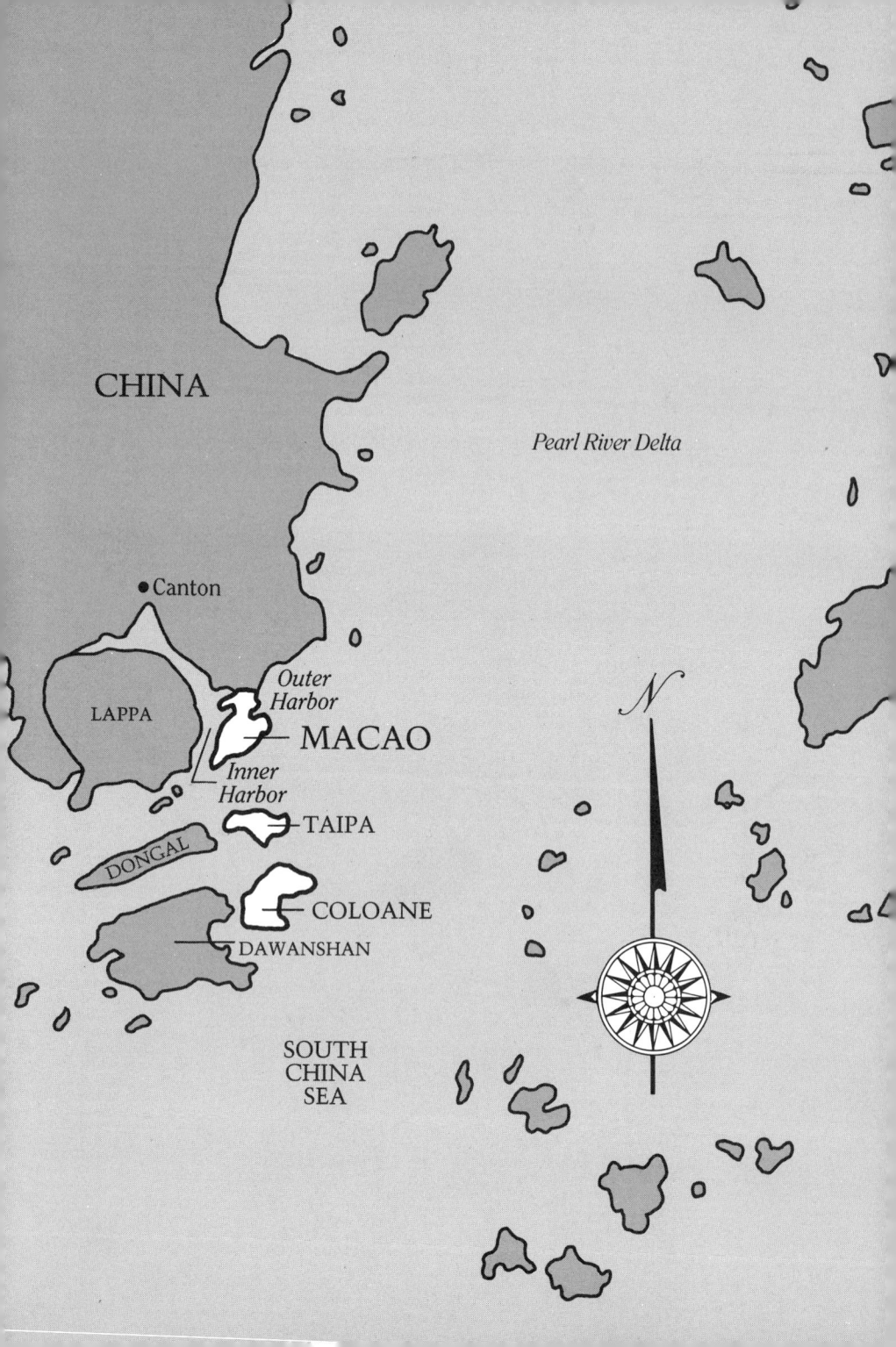

Pearl River Delta

• Canton

Outer Harbor

LAPPA

MACAO

Inner Harbor

TAIPA

DONGAL

COLOANE

DAWANSHAN

SOUTH CHINA SEA

N

CHINA

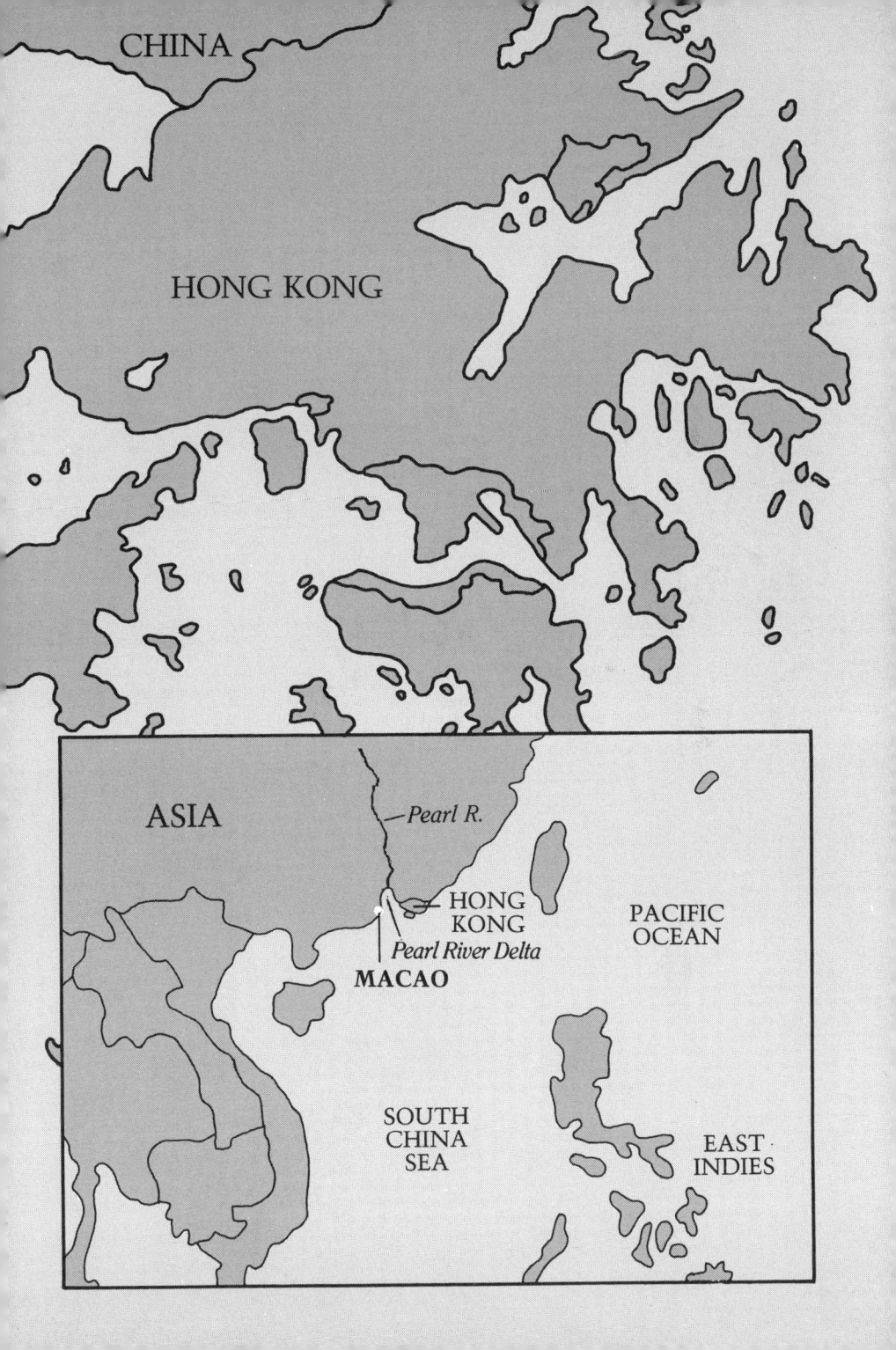

HONG KONG

ASIA — Pearl R. — HONG KONG — Pearl River Delta — **MACAO** — PACIFIC OCEAN — SOUTH CHINA SEA — EAST INDIES

◄ FACTS AT A GLANCE ►

Land and People

Area	6 square miles (16 square kilometers), including Taipa and Coloane
Highest Point	571 feet (171 meters) on Coloane Island
Population	450,000
Population Density	75,000 per square mile (28,125 per sq km)
Population Distribution	Urban, 99 percent; rural, 1 percent
Capital	Macao City
Official Language	Portuguese
Other Languages	Cantonese, English
Religions	Buddhist, 95 percent; Roman Catholic, 5 percent
Ethnic Groups	Chinese, 97 percent; Portuguese and Macanese (persons of mixed Asian and Portuguese descent), 3 percent

Economy

Sources of Income	Gambling, manufacturing, tourism
Industrial Products	Textiles, furniture, electronics, toys, porcelain, clothing
Major Resources	None
Major Trading Partners	China, Japan, United States
Currency	Patacá (8 patacás equal U.S. $1)
Average Annual Income	Equal to U.S. $1,000

Government

Form of Government	Autonomous territory of Portugal with an elected Legislative Assembly
Formal Head of State	President of Portugal
Head of Government	Governor, appointed by president

◄HISTORY AT A GLANCE►

before 1500   Chinese fishermen use Macao as a safe harbor during fishing trips.

1513   During a voyage from the Portuguese territory of Malacca to China, trader Jorge Álvares becomes the first European to sight the Macao peninsula and its surrounding islands.

1542   Portuguese trader Fernão Mendes Pinto lands in Japan. Portugal quickly establishes a monopoly on trade between Japan and China.

1557   China allows the Portuguese to establish a settlement in Macao. It quickly becomes a thriving trade center and the headquarters for the Christian missionary effort in Asia.

1580   Spain conquers Portugal and sends Spanish officials to direct Macao. Although trading continues, Dutch and Spanish ships begin to harass Macaon ships.

1604 to 1627   Dutch ships make repeated attempts to capture Macao, but they are unsuccessful.

1638   Fearing that missionaries are trying to undermine his rule, Japan's shogun (ruler) banishes all Christians and ends trade with Christian-dominated Macao.

1640   Portugal gains independence from Spain. Around the same time, China closes its port at Canton to Portuguese traders. Macao's great trade monopoly ends.

1700s	China opens Canton to European traders but allows them to live in the city only during the trading season. The rest of the year, the traders live in Macao, breathing some economic life back into the territory.
1821	China threatens to close Macao forever if Macaon traders deal in opium, a narcotic made from poppies. The Macaons heed this warning, but British traders continue to deal in the drug.
1839 to 1842	China and Great Britain clash in the Opium War. By the war's end, the British have gained control of Hong Kong, 40 miles (64 kilometers) from Macao. Hong Kong becomes a great commercial center, attracting most of Macao's merchants.
1844	In an attempt to revive its slumping economy, Macao legalizes gambling. Large casinos open, attracting thousands of gamblers.
1849	Macao's Portuguese governor closes the Chinese customs house after China refuses to give Portugal written control of Macao. Officials in the Chinese city of Canton offer a reward for the governor's death, and he is assassinated. In response, Macao captures a Chinese fort north of the Barrier Gate.
1887	After years of strained relations, Portugal and China finally sign a treaty in which China grants Portugal sovereignty over Macao.
1900	Thousands of refugees from China's Boxer Rebellion escape to Macao.
mid-1920s	China's civil war sends many more refugees into Macao.
late 1930s to 1945	During World War II, Japan attacks China and other Asian countries. Refugees flee to Macao, which shares Portugal's neutral status in the war. The tiny territory's population soars.

1949 A Communist revolution takes place in China. Another flood of refugees pours into Macao.

1966 China's Cultural Revolution (a campaign to rid China of people who oppose its Communist government) spurs riots that spill into Macao. Portugal offers to return Macao to China, but the offer is refused.

1974 A Socialist revolution shakes Portugal. The new government again offers to return Macao to Chinese control, but once again the offer is refused.

1976 Macao's status is changed from that of a "Portuguese overseas province" to a "Chinese territory under Portuguese administration."

1984 Macao's Chinese citizens gain voting rights.

late 1980s Chinese and Portuguese negotiators begin discussions about returning Macao to China.

The Barrier Gate is the only official crossing point from Macao into the People's Republic of China. The first gate was built in 1573.

Macao and the World

The territory of Macao is made up of a small peninsula on the Chinese coast and two neighboring islands. Located at the mouth of the Pearl River, about 70 miles (113 kilometers) from the Chinese city of Canton, Macao was once a safe harbor for Chinese fishermen. In 1557, it was settled by traders from the European nation of Portugal, which had established a monopoly on trade between China and Japan. Today, as a "Chinese territory administered by Portugal," it is a land caught between capitalism and communism, between its long Chinese heritage and hundreds of years of European tradition.

Only 6 square miles (16 square kilometers) in area, Macao is dwarfed by the vastness of China, which lies to the north. But the tiny territory was once the site of the most important trading post in Asia, a center of commerce between Europe, Japan, China, and the East Indies. Ships sailed into Macao bearing loads of Indonesian spices, and sailed out with cargoes of Chinese silks and Persian rugs. Macao's ports sent vessels loaded with European finery to Japan; when the ships returned, their holds were bulging with Japanese silver. Macao also served as the base for a Christian missionary effort in Asia. Catholic monks built churches and monasteries on the peninsula and sent missionaries throughout Asia.

By the early 1600s, Macao was a wealthy and cosmopolitan community. But this golden era was short-lived. Soon, Spain, Great Britain, and the Netherlands began fighting Portugal for trading rights, and Asian leaders grew suspicious of the missionary effort. By 1842, a series of Portuguese defeats and diplomatic setbacks had changed Macao from the center of Asian trade to the battered relic of a bygone era.

Macao underwent some desperate times after the collapse of its trading monopoly. But the Macaons did not give up. Instead, they looked for new ways to revitalize their economy. In 1844, Macaon officials legalized gambling, and people flocked to Macao to enjoy its casinos.

Every inch of space on the narrow peninsula of Macao is densely crowded.

In the early 20th century, people poured into Macao for another reason: to flee war. The territory became a haven for people fleeing China's Boxer Rebellion in 1900, its civil war in the 1920s, and World War II in the 1940s. By 1949, more than 500,000 people were crowded into the tiny territory. Today, the population is just over 450,000 people, making Macao the most densely populated area on the face of the earth.

Macao's large population supports itself with the revenue from its system of legalized gambling, for which it is unique in Asia. Light industry, such as the manufacture of clothing, toys, and furniture provides additional sources of support. Tourism also is becoming an important economic force. The once beleaguered territory now has a trade surplus and uses the extra money it earns from exports to build new roads, improve its harbors, and modernize health care.

Despite these bright economic statistics, however, many Macaons have a low standard of living. Most work as laborers in manufacturing plants and earn less for a day's work than many people in the United States make in one hour. They live in small shacks on the outskirts of the city of Macao or on small boats offshore. The government hopes that providing more education will help these people improve their lives.

A full 97 percent of Macao's people are of Chinese descent, and they follow traditional Chinese customs and ways of life. As a result, Macao blends the Mediterranean heritage of its Portuguese government with the Asian traditions of its Chinese citizens. Buddhist temples stand next to Catholic churches, and government-sponsored holidays include the Chinese New Year and the Feast of St. John the Baptist.

Although European influence remains strong, the Portuguese are prepared to give up their claim to Macao. In 1986, talks began between Portugal and China to determine Macao's fate. Hong Kong, a British territory to the east of Macao, will be returned to Chinese control in 1997. The Portuguese have agreed to surrender their Chinese colony as well; on December 20, 1999, control of Macao will return to China.

Many people in Macao are concerned about the impending change in government. Thousands of them are refugees from China. Some came to Macao in 1949, when the Communist party took control of China. Thousands more slipped into Macao during the many violent upheavals that took place in China after the revolution. These people fear that Chinese rule will jeopardize their freedom.

Others fear that the change in government will destroy Macao's economy. The Chinese operate under the Communist system, in which the government owns all businesses. Macao's economy, on the other hand, is based on private ownership, in which individuals or groups of individuals own and operate companies for their own profit. Many people worry that when China takes over Macao, it will seize private businesses and destroy Macao's profitable manufacturing trade.

China has assured the Macaons that these fears are unfounded. In recent years, the Chinese government has shifted away from strict communism toward a much more open society. Chinese leaders have stated that when they assume control of Macao, they will allow life to continue much as it always has.

Macao hopes to become once again a center of trade between China and the rest of the world. Even when it comes under Chinese rule at the end of the century, Macao is expected to carry on the tradition of trading that began more than 400 years ago.

The colony's history began with the sea. Today, many Macaons make their homes in a variety of junks, sampans, and fishing boats anchored in the Inner Harbor.

A Coastal Outpost

Macao is located on the southern coast of China at the mouth of the Pearl River (called the Chu Chaing-k'ou in Chinese). Lying about 70 miles (113 kilometers) south of the Chinese city of Canton, the territory includes the Macao peninsula and two nearby islands, Taipa and Coloane. Twenty miles (32 kilometers) to the east, across the surging brown waters of the Pearl River, rises the big Chinese island of Lantau, part of the British territory of Hong Kong. To the southeast, out in the middle of the river, are the Ladrones Islands, once the base of Chinese pirates. Further south lies the South China Sea.

Macao lies in an area known as the Pearl River Delta, where soil deposited by the river's flow has created land masses. The peninsula and the surrounding islands are composed largely of rocky outcroppings of granite. From the air, the delta looks like a twisting maze of waterways dotted with rocky islands. In fact, it is one large river containing hundreds of islands.

Although it shares a border with China, Macao is not considered a part of the Chinese mainland. The peninsula is actually part of the island of Hsiang Shan. Today, only sparse grasses and a few trees cover the peninsula and the islands. The area was once thick with subtropical forests, but they were destroyed centuries ago by Chinese foraging for firewood. Although the territory is surrounded by the brown waters of the Pearl River, Macao has no rivers or streams of its own. Therefore, all of its drinking water must be imported from China.

Only 2 square miles (5.2 square kilometers) in area, the Macao peninsula is made up of seven rocky hills. The two highest hills are known as Penha and Guia. From their summits, visitors can look west to the Chinese island of Lappa. The city of Macao covers the entire peninsula. Almost every inch of it is paved or built upon. Shops, factories, and homes—both large estates and small shacks—blanket Macao's hills. Occasional gardens and temple grounds provide the only greenery.

Macao is the most densely populated area on earth. Several years ago, the Macaon government initiated a landfill project (a program in which a body of water is filled with soil to create a land area) to expand the peninsula. As a result, its shallow eastern shore, known as the Porto Exterior (Outer Harbor), has been enlarged. A breakwater (a large, offshore wall) protects the harbor from storms that sweep in from the South China Sea.

The Porto Exterior is nearly filled with silt carried in by the river, which prevents it from accommodating large ships. On the other side, protected by the peninsula from the main flow of the Pearl River, lies the Porto Interior, or Inner Harbor. It was once a huge trading port, but today only small fishing boats can navigate it.

A 1.5-mile (2.4-kilometer) bridge links Macao with the island of Taipa. Once a peaceful, undeveloped place dotted with small shacks, the island now has factories, homes, and a few vacation resorts. With an area of 1.5 square miles (3.9 square kilometers), it is the smallest of Macao's land areas.

A long road built on a landfill connects Taipa to Coloane. Although it is the largest of Macao's land masses—some 2.5 square miles (6.5 square kilometers) in area—Coloane remains largely undeveloped. City dwellers from Macao and Taipa come to the quiet island to enjoy its unspoiled beaches and lush pine groves.

Climate

Macao has two seasons: summer and winter. The summer months, from April to September, are marked by high humidity and periodic typhoons (destructive tropical storms). During the winter, from October through March, the weather is cool and dry.

Summer temperatures usually reach more than 80° Fahrenheit (27° Centigrade) and are accompanied by humidity of 80 percent or more. During these months, great typhoons often strike Macao. (The word comes from the Chinese words *ta-fung*, meaning "great wind.") The Macaons know from experience how to tell when a typhoon is approaching. The clouds grow thick, the air becomes still and oppressive, and the sky turns yellow. Then the earth is fanned by warm, deceptively soft winds. Soon, however, the winds increase until they shriek across the land, carrying blinding sheets of rain in their wake.

The winds and rain of a typhoon can cause great damage. Anything that is not securely tied down can be swept away by the storm. Many Macaon homes are nothing more than bamboo shacks with flimsy tin roofs, and a typhoon can demolish them. The force of the winds can even wash an entire hillside neighborhood into the river.

Fortunately, the typhoon season passes. At the end of September, Macao begins its winter season, during which the weather is quite pleasant. It rains very little, the skies are clear and blue, and the temperature usually hovers around 60° F (15° C).

Searching for spices and other treasures, Portuguese explorers opened much of Asia to the West. This statue honors Jorge Álvares, who discovered Macao in 1513.

A History of Trade

The tiny peninsula of Macao seems an unlikely place to capture and hold the attention of powerful nations. But Macao was once the site of perhaps the richest trading center in the East. In fact, merchant ships from Portugal, Spain, Great Britain, and the Netherlands once fought one another—and the Chinese—for the right to trade with the rich port.

Long before Europeans even began exploring Asia, however, Macao was important. Chinese fishermen used it as a safe harbor between the peninsula's protective arm and the mainland. Although few fishermen settled on the peninsula, they built two ancient temples that still stand today. At the northern end of Macao, a temple honors Kuan Yin, the Chinese goddess of mercy. At the southern end, surrounded by large boulders and banyan trees, stands the A-Ma temple, from which Macao got its name.

Originally a small shrine, the A-Ma temple was built by fishermen from China's Fukian province. According to legend, the men were fishing in the Pearl River when a storm came up and almost capsized their boat. They prayed to the goddess A-Ma, the protector of fishermen, to save their lives, and were eventually blown into the peninsula's quiet inner harbor. The grateful fishermen built a shrine to honor the goddess who had saved them, and when Portuguese settlers arrived in Macao in the 16th century, they translated the Chinese "A-Ma" to Amacão or Amagão, later shortening it to Macao.

The development of Macao and its fabulously rich trade with China grew out of the great era of Portuguese exploration that began in the final years of the 15th century. In 1498, Portugal's Vasco da Gama sailed around Africa, discovering a sea route to India. He returned from India with tales of great wealth and with enough exotic spices to make himself instantly rich. Other Portuguese explorers soon followed his lead. By the early 1500s, Portugal had established colonies in Africa, India, and Malacca (a peninsula south of Thailand), as well as in Indonesia, then known as the Spice Islands.

The Portuguese traders had at first been attracted to the Far East for its spices. But after the Chinese brought their silks, musk, porcelain, and other riches to trade in Malacca, the Portuguese be-

The A-Ma temple, near the Inner Harbor, is Macao's oldest Chinese temple.

came interested in more than spices. In 1513, trader Jorge Álvares followed some Chinese ships back to their homeland. During the voyage, he discovered Macao.

The Portuguese were not interested in Macao at first. They were eager to exploit the riches they had found in China, and sent an ambassador there in 1515 to sign an official trading agreement with the Chinese government. The Chinese, however, refused to sign. Nevertheless, Portuguese ships went on trading illegally at small ports along the Chinese coast. They even established a small settlement on a coastal island. Then, in 1542, a junk (a small Chinese ship) bearing Portuguese trader Fernão Mendes Pinto and a friend was blown far off course. When the skies cleared, they found themselves in a strange new land—Japan.

The emperors of China had long forbidden trade with Japan because they distrusted the Japanese. But Japan was willing to pay high prices in silver for Chinese goods, especially silks. Despite the initial reluctance of Chinese authorities, the Portuguese soon became the middlemen in trade between China and Japan. By 1555, they were making regular visits between Canton and Japanese ports.

To make this trade practical, the Portuguese needed a permanent settlement near Canton. In 1557, China finally agreed to rent Portugal the rights to build on the tiny Macao peninsula, only 70 miles (113 kilometers) from Canton. Scholars believe that China allowed the Portuguese settlement for two reasons. First, the Portuguese had defeated several pirate junks that had been harassing Cantonese ships. Second, the Chinese felt they could conduct a prosperous trade with the Portuguese while at the same time keeping them under control on the tiny peninsula. To emphasize that the Portuguese were *yang kuei,* or "foreign devils," the Chinese erected the Barrier Gate at the north end of the peninsula to keep them out of China. A gate still stands there today to separate the Portuguese settlement from the Chinese mainland.

A Thriving Settlement

Macao's founding fathers quickly established a prosperous community. Enriched by the growing trade with Japan, these first settlers built spacious houses along cobblestoned streets. Macao's Chinese inhabitants also prospered. The Portuguese employed Chinese fishermen to build new, large sailing ships; they also bought ducks, eggs, pigs, and fresh vegetables from farmers in the surrounding countryside. The territory flourished.

Soon, Macao became the center of the Catholic church's missionary effort in the East. Portuguese monks flocked to the island, hoping to convert all of Asia. As a result, churches were among the first and largest Portuguese construction projects in Macao. By the late 1500s, people sailing into Macao's outer harbor might have imagined themselves not in China but back on the Mediterranean coast. Graceful stone houses and rounded church domes, surrounded by trees and bright flower gardens, rose on the seven hills. The settlement's centerpiece was the gracefully soaring cathedral of São Paulo (St. Paul), considered the greatest monument to Christianity in the East. Its construction was funded by European monarchs.

From its founding in 1557 until about 1640, Macao experienced a golden era. It had a virtual monopoly on trade between China and Japan and continued to ship rich cargoes back to Portugal. It received ships loaded with pepper, nutmeg, and cinnamon from Malacca and sent cargoes of Chinese silks, Persian carpets, and European mirrors to Japan. Ships returned from Japan loaded with barrels full of silver.

Ironically, Macao's very wealth set the stage for its decline. In the late 1500s, Spain established control of the Philippines and was anxious to take a cut of Portugal's trade with Japan and China. In 1580, Spain conquered Portugal and sent Spanish officials to direct its colonies, including Malacca and Macao. (The Macaons largely

Catholic missionaries in the East, like this Jesuit priest, were based in Macao.

ignored their Spanish overlords, however, and Portugal gained independence from Spain in 1640.) Meanwhile, the Netherlands, with a large and powerful navy, was pushing its way into the region. Dutch ships made several attempts to capture Macao, but were unsuccessful. Nevertheless, Dutch ships continued to harass and capture Macaon ships. Spanish ships also raided Macaon cargoes.

In addition to this pressure, Macao faced more trouble from Japan. In the 1630s, Japan's shogun (ruler) became convinced that Christian missionaries were attempting to overthrow him. After Japanese Christians staged an uprising in Nagasaki in 1638, the shogun ordered the murder of thousands of Christians. Thousands more were expelled from Japan. In 1640, Macao sent a 60-man mission to Japan to plead for the Christians; the shogun responded by executing the party. Relations between Japan and Macao were destroyed, and Macao's great trade monopoly had ended.

A Territory in Trouble

The end of the trade monopoly was only the beginning of Macao's troubles. In 1640, China closed Canton to Portuguese traders, and one year later the Dutch captured Malacca. The Macaon settlers were virtually cut off from their homeland by hostile Dutch ships. A Dutch-Portuguese truce in 1644 allowed the Macaons to resume enough trade to support themselves, but the next 60 years were often desperate.

The situation improved in the early 1700s, as Great Britain and other countries expanded trade with China. Because authorities in the Chinese city of Canton allowed foreigners to remain in their city only during the trading months (between November and May), traders needed a place to live during the rest of the year. They chose Macao, bringing renewed life to the once-dominant trading outpost.

Soon, however, international trade wars again threatened Macao's prosperity. By the 19th century, Great Britain had created a profitable business by shipping opium (a narcotic drug extracted from poppies) from India into China. At first, Macaon merchants joined in the drug trading. But Chinese officials strongly opposed the opium trade, and in 1821 they made it clear that they would close Macao forever if it dealt in opium. Macao's traders heeded this warning and stopped trading in drugs.

British opium smuggling continued, however. Chinese attempts to stop it resulted in the Opium War, which lasted from 1839 to 1842. With its superior weapons, England forced the Chinese government to sign the Treaty of Nanking, which allowed Great Britain free trade in Canton and—more importantly—gave them ownership of a small island and harbor called Hong Kong, 40 miles (64 kilometers) east of Macao. The establishment of a British colony there marked the end of Macao's long-lasting control of the China trade. Within a few years, Macao's leading merchants had moved their operations to Hong Kong.

Despite this setback, Macao did not give up. Instead, it looked for new ways to revitalize its economy. In 1844, it legalized gambling, a move that brought in much income. And soon Portugal, which had never obtained formal rights to Macao, tried to get a firm hold on the colony by pressing China for an agreement.

The Opium War between China and Britain resulted in the establishment of the British colony of Hong Kong—and in Macao's subsequent loss of trade and importance.

Unfortunately for Macao, the Chinese government refused to sign a written agreement. The refusal began a long period of tension between China and the Portuguese territory. In retaliation for China's refusal, Macao's Portuguese governor closed the Chinese customs house, a major source of income for China, in 1849. Tensions peaked later that year, when Cantonese officials offered a reward for the death of the governor of Macao. Assassins killed him, and the stunned Macaons demanded retribution.

To strike back at the Cantonese government, Macaon soldiers captured a Chinese fort 1 mile (1.6 kilometers) north of the Barrier Gate. The British, who were equally horrified by the assassination, sent warships and marines from Hong Kong to prevent China from attacking Macao.

Relations between Macao and China remained strained until December 1887, when the two finally signed a treaty. China agreed

The Taipa Bridge links mainland Macao and the island of Taipa. It is 1.6 miles (2.5 kilometers) long.

to "the perpetual occupation and government of Macao and its dependencies by Portugal, as any other Portuguese possession."

For much of the first half of the 20th century, Macao served as a refuge for people leaving China. In 1900, during the Boxer Rebellion (a Chinese uprising against foreigners), hundreds of Chinese took refuge in Macao. During China's civil war in the mid-1920s, the city again took in thousands of refugees. Twenty years later, during World War II, refugees from throughout Japanese-occupied Asia flooded neutral Macao. Macao's population exploded to 500,000. After the war, China's Communist Revolution of 1949 sent another wave of refugees into tiny Macao.

Macao and the New China

Although the Chinese revolution drastically altered life in that country, the relationship between China and Macao did not change. Dur-

In 1966, Macaon students and workers carry posters of China's Chairman Mao at an anti-British demonstration.

ing the next two decades, life in Macao proceeded normally. In 1966, however, China's Cultural Revolution (a campaign to rid China of old ideas and practices that were contrary to the new communism) brought riots to Macao. Young Macaons who supported China's Communist government demonstrated in the streets, chanting, "Kill the Portuguese devils," and some rioters wrecked Portuguese administrative buildings in Macao City.

In response to these massive demonstrations, the Portuguese offered to return Macao to China. But Chinese leaders, fearing that taking over the territory would create an economic panic in Hong Kong (a British colony 40 miles (64 kilometers) west of Macao), refused the offer. China depended on Hong Kong for more than U.S. $600 million in revenue each year, and economic turmoil there could have greatly weakened China's own economy.

Portugal experienced its own revolution in 1974, and its new Socialist government again offered to return Macao to Chinese control. The offer was again refused. However, in 1976, Portugal signed an agreement with China that changed Macao's status from that of a Portuguese "overseas province" to "Chinese territory under Portuguese administration."

In 1984, Great Britain signed an agreement to return Hong Kong to China in 1997. Shortly thereafter, China turned its attention back to Macao. Although they had refused two previous offers to take over the territory, Chinese leaders now pressed Portugal to set a date for returning Macao to their control. In 1986, negotiations began, and in April 1987, Portugal declared that it would give Macao back to China on December 20, 1999.

Today, Macao stands as a relic of Portugal's once-fabulous role in Asian trade. But it has also made a place for itself in the modern world. During the 1970s, it began rebuilding its trade economy. With the help of money from Hong Kong investors, it built dozens of factories to produce textiles for export. Today, the territory earns millions by selling clothing, furniture, toys, electronics, and other products to nations around the world. Even after it comes under Chinese control at the end of the century, it is expected to remain an important trading center.

Parts of this temple dedicated to Kuan Yin, the goddess of mercy, are covered with porcelain panels from China's Ming dynasty.

A Rich Culture

Macao was once a barren refuge for fishermen from mainland China. When the Portuguese arrived, only a few shacks dotted the territory. But today, approximately 450,000 people live in Macao. This huge population is jammed into 6 square miles (16 square kilometers), making Macao the most crowded territory on earth with an average of 75,000 people per square mile (28,125 per sq km).

Not surprisingly, then, space is at a premium. A 1981 survey showed that the average household has 5.8 persons, and that nearly one-fourth of Macao's families have to share their living quarters with other families. An estimated 15 percent of all adults live in squatter shacks or huts, and another 5 percent make their homes on fishing junks. Others, however, live in large, two-story stone houses built by early settlers on the flats facing the inner harbor. In the early years, the upper stories of these homes, with their high ceilings and tall, narrow windows, served as the living quarters, and the ground floors were used primarily to store supplies.

Ninety-seven percent of Macao's citizens are Chinese; the other 3 percent include Portuguese (most of whom work for the government), foreign businessmen of many nationalities, and Macanese (persons of mixed Portuguese and Asian ancestry). Throughout Macao, the combination of Chinese and European influences is evident. For example, European business people dress in Western clothing, but the Chinese, long accustomed to the heat and high humidity of this semitropical region, generally wear dark, loose-fitting clothing for everyday wear. Both men and women commonly wear pants because they are the most practical work clothes. In the past, many women wore Malayan blouses (called *kains*) and robes (called *kabayas*); they placed light shawls over their heads and shoulders as protection against the sun and to cover their faces when in the presence of strangers. This practice, however, is no longer common.

Although Macao's official language is Portuguese, less than 4 percent of the population speaks it. The dominant language is Cantonese, the dialect of southern China. English is also quite widely spoken, especially by the younger, better-educated Macaons. A 1981 survey showed that about 16 percent of Macao's total population could speak English, but that more than 31 percent of those between the ages of 15 and 19 could speak it.

Macao's cuisine reflects more than 400 years of Portuguese-Chinese relations. The Portuguese taught the Chinese to grow sweet potatoes as a winter crop and introduced them to peanuts, which they used to make peanut oil (it is the primary vegetable cooking oil in China today). The Portuguese also gave the Chinese hot peppers and fruits, such as papayas and pineapples. But the Portuguese received new foods from the Chinese as well: such Oriental crops as celery and rhubarb, and a dwarf orange tree that they planted in Tangier, Morocco. It later became known in Europe as the tangerine.

Portugal's glory days as a world colonial power can still be tasted in the dishes of Macao. For example, prawns (a type of shrimp) heavily spiced with chilis and other peppers can be traced to Gôa in India, once an important stop on Portugal's trade route. Portuguese exploration in Brazil contributed *feijoadas*—a stew of pork, spicy sausage, beans, cabbage, and potatoes—to Macao's menu. The territory's most famous dish, African chicken (made by marinating chicken in a garlic, pepper, and chili sauce, then grilling it), came to Macao after the Portuguese explored the African continent. Portuguese wines, which are abundant and inexpensive, complement most meals, making dining in Macao a truly international experience.

Religion and Holidays

Chinese and European religious practices have existed side by side in Macao ever since the Portuguese arrived in the 1500s. The spirit of religious tolerance begun centuries ago continues in modern-day Macao. Religious prejudice is uncommon. Buddhist temples sit next

This Chinese-style altar features a statue of Buddha, who lived in the 6th century B.C. Most of Macao's inhabitants are followers of the Buddhist faith.

to Catholic cathedrals, and all Macaons enjoy the celebrations of both cultures.

Macao's principal religions are Buddhism and Roman Catholicism. Buddhists, who make up 95 percent of Macao's population, follow the teachings of Siddhartha Gautama, known as Buddha (the Enlightened One). Siddhartha lived in northern India from about 563 B.C. to 483 B.C. According to belief, he became Buddha at the age of 35 after he spent all night meditating underneath a pipal tree. His teachings stress that good thoughts bring good results and evil thoughts bring bad results. Buddha also believed that people should avoid extremes, following instead a "middle path."

As practiced in Macao, Buddhism is often mixed with the teachings of two ancient Chinese philosophers, Lao-tzu and Confucius. Lao-tzu, who lived during the 6th century B.C., created the philosophy of the Tao (pronounced "dow"), which means "the way." Based on Lao-tzu's book, the *Tao Te Ching*, Taoism stresses that every natural occurrence has an opposite and that a thing and its opposite are equal in strength. Day and night, hot and cold, and good and evil are opposites, but each one grows from and complements the other. Confucius, who lived from 551 B.C. to 479 B.C., was one of China's greatest philosophers. His teachings combined politics and morality. He urged people to learn from the past and to honor their parents and ancestors. As a result, many Chinese in Macao honor their ancestors through prayers and regularly tend the graves of their forebears.

Other ancient Chinese beliefs have also remained a part of Macao's culture. For example, temples dedicated to various gods are found throughout the territory. The most famous of these is the temple of Kuan Yin, the goddess of mercy. Monks flock to the shrine to honor her with prayers and incense. Another shrine, the temple of A-Ma, is thought to be the oldest in Macao. It is dedicated to the patron goddess of sailors, for whom the city is named. The temple's

(continued on page 49)

SCENES OF
MACAO

➤ *Coloane Island's beaches amid warm waters attract many tourists.*

➤ *Incense rises in a cloud from one of the buildings of the ancient A-Ma temple.*

▲ Undeveloped Coloane still has lush, quiet forests.

▼ Taipa Island's shores are rocky and rugged.

▲ *Rapid jetfoil boats skim between Macao and Hong Kong.*

◄ *Many foods come across the border from China.*

▼ *The dragon dance at the Kuan Yin temple is traditional.*

⋏ The Dragon Boat Races are one of Macao's liveliest festivals.

➤ *The great stone facade is all that remains of St. Paul's Cathedral.*

◂ *Catholic worship continues in this São Domingo church.*

▲ The Border Gate may no longer be needed once Macao is returned to China.

▼ Viewed from Guia Fortress, the city presents a panorama of old and new.

▼ Rickshaws jostle cars on busy streets.

➤ The Bishop's Palace crowns the summit of Penha Hill, one of the territory's two highest points.

▼ Student guides at Monte Fort are wearing 18th-century Portuguese uniforms.

(continued from page 40)

grounds house shrines to Kuan Yin and other Chinese gods as well. In the Lin Fong temple near the Macao-China border, people pray to the statues of a variety of ancient Chinese gods, each of whom has a "specialty," such as improving crops, business, or health.

Macao's citizens participate in a number of Chinese and local festivals. Young and old alike eagerly anticipate these events, which are carried out in much the same way as they have been for centuries. Of many traditional festivals, three of the biggest are the Dragon Boat Festival, the Mooncake Festival, and the Chinese New Year.

The Dragon Boat Festival, called the Wu Yueh Chieh (Fifth Moon Festival) by the Chinese, is always celebrated on the fifth day of the fifth month of the Chinese calendar. The festival celebrates the dragon, which is believed to control water and to bring the rains that fall at the end of the fifth month. In southern China and Macao, the Wu Yueh Chieh is celebrated with boat races that commemorate the death of Ch'u Yuan, a revered 4th-century B.C. government official who drowned.

The sleek dragon boats used in the festival are 60 to 120 feet (18 to 36 meters) long and are operated by dozens of paddlers. The boats are very shallow and can easily be overturned if the paddlers are not careful. During the race, the leader of each boat sits in his boat's bow beating a large drum and shouting frenzied encouragement to his crew.

On shore, people in the crowd spend as much time watching each other as the races. Spectators drink many cups of tea and eat a special delicacy called *ch'un tze*, a mixture of sticky rice, pork, lotus seeds, and boiled egg yolks wrapped in bamboo leaves. Traditionally, each ch'un tze is wrapped in five leaves and tied with silk threads of five different colors to represent the fifth moon.

Another important celebration is the Mooncake Festival, which occurs during the eighth moon of the Chinese calendar year. It is

Women took part in the annual Dragon Boat Races for the first time in 1970. The festival honors Ch'u Yuan, a Chinese official who drowned centuries ago.

comparable to the harvest moon festival celebrated by farmers in some Western countries. In Macao, it takes place when the last of the crops are taken in by the light of the full moon. The festival represents the seasonal shift from the hot, sunny days of summer (known to the Chinese as *yang* or the masculine part of the year) to the cool and dark winter (called *yin*, or the feminine part of the year). During the festival, bakery shops turn out thousands of "mooncakes"—light, sugary buns filled with sweetened bean paste, lotus or sesame seeds, and sometimes pork. On the festival day, virtually all Chinese eat the buns, which are golden in color, like the moon.

By far the most important festival in Macao is the Chinese New Year. The time of the celebration is based on the lunar calendar, which originated more than 3,000 years ago. According to this calendar, New Year's Day changes each year but always falls between January 21 and February 19 on the Julian calendar.

As New Year's Day approaches, the Chinese traditionally rush to settle all outstanding debts so they can start the new year with a clean slate. They put small amounts of money into red envelopes (red is considered a lucky color) and give them to children and servants. They cover their entrance doorways with red paper inscribed with Chinese sayings, such as "May your entering and departure be peaceful."

About a week before New Year's Day, people pay special attention to Tsao Wang, the kitchen god. In many houses, a statue of Tsao Wang is kept in the kitchen on a small altar. According to belief, Tsao Wang sees all of the family's activities throughout the year, and on New Year's Eve he travels to heaven to report them to the gods. Before he leaves, family members smear the statue's lips with honey to ensure that he will say only sweet things about them.

All the food eaten on New Year's Day is prepared in advance. No cooking is done on this day because many believe that if a family member cuts himself with a knife, the family's luck could be slashed. Wealthy families wear new clothes on New Year's Day, then proceed to the streets, where they perform a traditional lion dance and set off firecrackers to frighten away evil spirits.

Another New Year's tradition is visiting temples and placing food and fruit on the altars to thank the gods for their favors. A wealthy family might place an entire roasted suckling pig on the altar. Near the temples, people assemble around small, makeshift stages made from bamboo that are erected for performances of Chinese opera. The opera's actors wear bright costumes and paint their faces with strange and colorful patterns that reveal whether the character is good or bad. The operas tell ancient stories of kings, bandits, and ladies in distress and teach that righteous people will overcome cruel landlords or emperors. The songs that the actors sing are often allegories (stories in which the actions of fictional characters reveal truths about human nature).

Although only 5 percent of Macao's population is Catholic, the church's influence remains strong, and the Macaons celebrate many Catholic holidays. For example, in late February, Macao holds the Procession of Our Lord of Passos. During this celebration, the faithful carry a statue of Christ on the cross through Macao's streets, then hold an all-night vigil, followed by another procession in the morning. June brings the Feast of St. John the Baptist (the city's patron saint), which has been celebrated in Macao ever since the Portuguese repelled a Dutch attack on the territory in 1622.

A statue of Christ is carried through the city streets in the Procession of Our Lord of Passos. The procession takes place each February.

Family Traditions

In addition to festivals, other ancient Chinese traditions also continue into the present. These are especially evident in family life. Even today, some parents arrange their children's marriages—the bride and groom have nothing to say about it. The families also commonly consult an astrologer to see if the horoscopes of a prospective couple are compatible.

To determine compatibility, the astrologer first examines the bride and groom's birth dates. According to the Chinese calendar, each year is associated with a certain animal, such as an ox, dragon, or snake. Some animals are considered to be incompatible. For example, "the boar and the monkey are soon parted" is one saying. Therefore, if the bride was born in the year of the boar and the groom in the year of the monkey, the astrologer would warn that they could not live in harmony.

If the astrologer confirms the marriage, the family then turns to a soothsayer (fortune-teller) to select the best day for a wedding. Many Chinese believe that a soothsayer can determine which days will bring good fortune to the newlyweds and which will be unlucky for them.

Just as Chinese marriage traditions continue in Macao, so do funeral traditions. Funeral arrangements begin when a deceased person's family consults the soothsayer to determine the best day for the burial. After a day has been selected, someone hollows a huge coffin out of a single large log that has been lacquered and painted. On the day of the funeral, mourners dressed all in white begin a procession through the streets toward the gravesite. A band playing funeral marches accompanies the procession, which includes family, friends, and professional mourners who are hired to weep and moan loudly. Banners carried on bamboo poles pay tribute to the deceased, and mourners throw play money into the air to distract any evil spirits who may be watching.

Art and Literature

History and ancient customs play an important role in Macao's culture. Many of the territory's art forms can be traced to age-old Chinese traditions, whereas other cultural events are linked to the European influences that cropped up in the area throughout Macao's history.

Luis Vaz de Camões, Portugal's most famous poet, stayed in Macao for a time. He may have written part of his great epic while roaming the harbor shores.

The European influence is evident in Macao's literary tradition. Portugal's most famous poet, Luís Vaz de Camões, is believed to have written part of his greatest epic poem during a stay in Macao. Born in Lisbon in 1524, de Camões' restless spirit took him to Macao in 1557, the year it was founded. For a brief period, he held the title of Official Responsible for the Property of Dead and Missing Portuguese—no small task in those times of piracy, typhoons, and disease.

During his stay, Camões roamed about the north end of the inner harbor, where a small hill dominated by a group of large, smooth rocks stood. Legend has it that Camões walked there regularly to contemplate the progress of his epic poem, *Os Lusiadas* (The Portuguese), which tells of the years of Portuguese discovery and conquest. In memory of the great poet, this area has been made into a quiet little park called the Rocks of Camões.

A museum on Macao also bears the poet's name. It houses a large collection of artistic and historic items, including paintings by the Chinese master Lam Qua and by Western painters George Smirnoff and Marciano Baptista, both of whom stayed in Macao. Some fine Chinese statues produced near Canton, known as Skekwan statuary, can also be seen here.

The Camões museum houses several works by another person of historical note in Macao—the artist George Chinnery. From 1825 until his death in 1852, Chinnery lived and worked in Macao, where he painted many portraits of the elite of Macao's society—Portuguese, English, and Chinese alike. The simple lines of his paintings capture the grace and mood of the territory in the mid-19th century.

Another historical figure who maintained close contact with Macao was Sun Yat-sen, who became the first president of China in 1911 following the overthrow of the Manchu dynasty. Born just 20 miles (32 kilometers) from Macao, Sun practiced medicine there for two years as a young man. Then, he returned to China to bring about the social changes that led to the Manchu dynasty's fall. Al-

Chinese men play a game called "elephant chess."

though he was forced from office a few years after taking over, he is still revered as the founder of modern China. The Sun Yat-sen Memorial House in Macao, a Moorish-style structure built on the site of the leader's original home, contains historic photographs and early writings about the revolution. Other exhibits tracing Macao's tumultuous history are found in the National Library, the Historical Archives, and the Military Museum.

Other Traditions

Gambling is an important part of the Chinese culture and is very popular in Macao. Most of Macao's gambling takes place in the five licensed casinos in the territory. Located in major hotels, the casinos are lavish, with huge rooms carpeted in red for good luck. The rooms glow with the flashing lights on slot machines, which the Chinese call "hungry tigers." The casinos offer the same gambling games that are popular in Western casinos—roulette, boule (a game similar to roulette), craps, baccarat, and blackjack.

The Chinese have their own games of chance as well. One of the most popular is *fan-tan*. In this ancient game, a pile of several hundred white porcelain beads is placed in the center of a table. A croupier (a person who operates a gambling game) plunges a silver cup upside down into the pile and slides the cup to the side of the table. Players then bet on how many beads will remain in the cup after they are divided by four. Chinese also play *dai sui*, or "big and small." In this game, three dice are thrown under a covered glass container. Players bet by guessing which numbers will come up on the dice.

The Avenida Almeida Ribeiro is Macao's main street. The whitewashed building on the left is the Leal Senado, home of the "Loyal Senate."

Land of Contrasts

The sights and sounds of Macao reflect its dual Chinese-Portuguese history. In the city of Macao, the ancient and the modern mix: centuries-old Chinese temples sit next to modern glass-and-steel high-rise buildings. In the sleepy towns on the outer islands, tiny village homes contrast with modern vacation hotels.

Macao City, only 2 square miles (5.2 square kilometers) in size, is the territory's hub. Founded in 1557, it abounds with evidence of Macao's long and colorful history. Even the layout of the streets tells a story. Macao was once surrounded by a huge defensive stone wall. Within the city's walls, narrow cobblestoned streets wound their way from place to place. As the city expanded, the wall was torn down. Today, the wall's former location is marked by places where the winding cobblestoned paths meet straight, modern roadways.

The Asian tradition of street vending continues, turning the city's thoroughfares into marketplaces. Vendors set up shop on the sidewalks to sell their wares, shouting to passersby about the quality of their merchandise. Street stalls contain baskets of fresh fruits and vegetables and buckets of live fish. Smoked ducks and slabs of pork hang in the windows of the shops that line the streets. Inside the stores, tables are laden with layers of dried and salted fish.

Much of the city's architecture reflects its Portuguese past. In the old quarters, houses are painted in the pastel shades that were popular in Portugal at the time of Macao's founding. These homes are styled in the Mediterranean fashion, with wooden shutters on the windows to keep out the afternoon sun and graceful balconies surrounded by wrought-iron railings. Behind the high walls that encircle the homes, peaceful gardens bloom with colorful flowers.

The greatest architectural landmark in Macao is the ruin of St. Paul's cathedral. Built around 1602 by Japanese Christians who had fled persecution in their country, it was once considered one of the most beautiful churches in the world. It burned to the ground in

The historic 17th-century facade of St. Paul's, once described as "the greatest monument to Christianity," is Macao's most famous landmark.

1835, however, and today all that remains is a sweeping stone stairway and a stone facade covered with intricate carvings.

The facade reveals something of Macao's long history. It is capped by the cross of Jerusalem. Below the cross sit three tiers of statues, cast in bronze at an early Macao cannon factory, that include a dove (representing the Holy Spirit), the Infant Jesus, the Virgin Mary, and angels. The Virgin Mary is flanked by two kinds of stone flowers—a chrysanthemum, representing Japan, and a peony, representing China. Other carvings on the facade include a demon, a Portuguese sailing ship, and the fountain of eternal life.

The cathedral is not the oldest structure in Macao. Jesuit missionaries built a fort called the Citadel of São Paulo de Monte at around the same time that St. Paul's was built. Monte Forte, as it is commonly called, is a large fortress near the center of the city. It is famous for its defense of the city during a 1622 attack by Dutch raiders, when a cannonball fired from the fort destroyed a Dutch ship.

Macao has other forts. One of the most imposing is the Guia fortress, on the city's highest hill. Complete with turrets and high walls, it was built between 1637 and 1638 to defend Macao from continuing Dutch attacks. The fortress contains the first lighthouse ever built on the Chinese coast. Using kerosene lamps and highly polished mirrors, it first cast its light across the South China Sea in September 1865. Although the original lamps have been replaced by modern electrical ones, the lighthouse still shines through the night.

European architecture is also evident in the Leal Senado building. Its inner courtyard, surrounded by blue-and-white tiled walls and capped by historic stone carvings, leads to a small, walled garden. The garden is marked by a grassy dome representing Portuguese exploration of the world. Beyond the garden lies the main Senate building, an ornate structure with heavily paneled walls and ceilings. In the Senate room, a long table stretches to a raised platform where

Built by Jesuit missionaries, Monte Fort is Macao's oldest structure.

the governor sits during sessions. The wall is inscribed with the city's motto: "City of the Name of God, Macao. There is None more loyal."

Another beautiful European-style building is the Teatro Dom Pedro V, Macao's principal theater for plays and symphonies. Built in 1872, it is considered as beautiful as many of Europe's finest theaters. It is noted for its circular main room and its cleverly disguised ceiling vents, which create a natural cooling effect that make the theater comfortable even on Macao's muggy summer evenings.

Just as these structures mark some of Macao's Portuguese heritage, numerous beautiful temples reflect its Chinese influence. The largest is the Temple of Kuan Yin (or Kum Iam), the goddess of mercy and queen of heaven. At least 400 years old, the temple is one of the oldest on Macao. Its entrance is marked by a large courtyard shaded by a spreading banyan tree. Two stone lions stand on each side of the stairs below the main doorway. Each lion holds a carved stone ball in its mouth; turning the ball three times to the left is said to bring good fortune. The temple's roof is covered with carved porcelain tiles, and its eaves and walls are decorated with porcelain figures of fish and dragons. These date from the Ming dynasty (about four centuries ago) and represent good luck.

Inside the temple are three altars, each higher than the one before. The first altar is dedicated to Buddha, and three gold-lacquer statues of him rest in glass cases on top of the altar. The second

In 1844, China and the United States signed their first treaty here in the Kuan Yin temple.

altar is dedicated to the Enlightened Buddha (Buddha after he reached spiritual purity), and his statue sits on a lotus blossom, a symbol of Buddhism. The final altar is for Kuan Yin. Her image, dressed in the robes of a Chinese bride, sits above the altar. Next to the altars stand gold lacquer figures of 18 wise men of China, including one figure with bulging eyes, a large nose, and a beard— the Italian explorer Marco Polo, the first European to travel to China.

Many Chinese come to this temple to have their fortunes told. Worshippers must first pay their respects to Kuan Yin by lighting some joss sticks (a type of incense). Then they select a bamboo container that holds about 20 thin bamboo slivers, each marked with a single Chinese character. The worshippers slowly shake the canister until one sliver falls out. They hand the sliver to an attendant, who gives them a piece of paper that matches the character on the sliver. The person's fortune for the day is written on the paper. Worshippers who do not like their fortunes may go back and repeat the process until they receive a better prophecy.

The temple is also famous as the site where China and the United States signed a treaty of trade and friendship in 1844. A round stone table surrounded by four stone benches sits in a small enclosed garden at the side of the temple. Kiying, governor of the Kwangtung province, and U.S. Ambassador Caleb Cushing sat at the table to sign the treaty.

Macao's oldest temple, the shrine to the goddess A-Ma, stands near the entrance to the Inner Harbor. The exact date of its construction is unknown, but it was built long before the Portuguese first sighted Macao in 1513. The rocks that surround the temple are covered with carvings. One rock, adorned with a picture of a Chinese junk, is said to have been carved by the fishermen who erected the shrine so many years ago.

Another historic area is the Old Protestant Cemetery, located behind high walls next to an old mansion. Visitors must ring a bell by the gate to gain admission to the cemetery, which is now a park. Ancient flowering trees grow among the weathered gravestones that mark the final resting places of many of Macao's most famous residents. Painter George Chinnery, missionary Robert Morrison (who compiled the first Chinese-English dictionary), and Captain Lord John Spencer Churchill, an ancestor of England's great prime minister Sir Winston Churchill, are all buried in the cemetery.

Little European influence has extended to Taipa and Coloane. Chinese villages and temples dot these islands, which remain relatively secluded. Difficulties in supplying electrical power and water have kept the islands from developing. The 20th century has recently begun to make inroads, however. Recent developments on Taipa include a large horse trotting track, several resort hotels, the University of East Asia, and a new town that houses 15,000 people.

The Loyal Senate was once an important assembly. Today, it acts as a municipal council and manages the routine affairs of the city.

Government and Social Services

Macao's governmental structure has remained virtually the same for more than four centuries. Ever since the first settlers established their trading colony in 1557, local authorities have managed Macao's affairs while answering to Portugal's central government in Lisbon.

Today, this system continues in Macao. The president of Portugal appoints Macao's governor for an unspecified term (usually four years, although it may be longer). The governor's job is to administer laws imposed by Macao's 17-member Legislative Assembly. Five members of the committee are appointed by the governor and 12 are elected to office. Macao's citizens also elect one member to Portugal's legislature, the National Assembly.

In government and financial matters, the governor and the Legislative Assembly are assisted by the Advisory Council. Two appointed members, three elected members, and three observers make up the council. The council's leader is usually a powerful Chinese businessman and is always a member of China's National People's Congress. Through him, China gains the power to veto any law or policy proposed by the Advisory Council. The Leal Senado, or Loyal Senate, was once Macao's most important assembly. Today, it acts as the municipal council, taking care of routine matters in the city.

All leading officials in the Macaon government are appointed by Portugal. Most of their top assistants are Portuguese, although many were born in Macao. For many years, only Portuguese or Macaons of Portuguese descent were allowed to vote, but Macao's Chinese citizens gained voting rights in 1984.

Of course, this political system will change rapidly when Portugal turns Macao over to Chinese control in 1999. Although the Chinese have assured the Macaons that they will not make major changes in the territory's economic and social systems, the shift in goverment is bound to alter life in Macao. Certainly, it will change the nation's leadership and the way government officials are selected.

Education

Education is highly valued in Macao, and 80 percent of Macaons over age ten can read and write. Macao's educational system, administered by the Chinese government, consists of primary, secondary, and college-level instruction. Both public and private schools operate in Macao.

Children are required to attend five years of primary school. At age 11, they may begin up to five years of secondary education, although this is not required by law. After secondary school, students who choose to may attend the University of East Asia, the only university in the territory. Opened in March 1981 on the island of Taipa, it provides a four-year education. Courses, taught primarily in English, emphasize mathematics and the sciences, but other subjects also are studied. Hotel management and textile development, which support two of Macao's most important industries, are popular courses of study at the university.

Health

One of Macao's most pressing problems is health care. In 1986, the territory had just 554 doctors for its 450,000 citizens—only 1 doctor

The University of East Asia, which opened in 1981, is the territory's only university.

for every 812 people. Although this was a great improvement over the situation of 1966, when Macao had only 78 doctors, more medical professionals are needed.

The doctor shortage is eased somewhat by practitioners of traditional Chinese medicine. Macao has 254 such healers who treat patients using herbal medicines and acupuncture. For centuries, Chinese doctors have used the acupuncture process, in which thin needles are inserted into the skin at various points of the body, to relieve pain. Other health-care professionals, including nurses and midwives (people trained to help women deliver babies), also practice in Macao.

The nuns of Santa Casa da Misericordia have cared for orphans for nearly five centuries.

Health-care facilities include a government hospital, two Catholic hospitals, two clinics, and dozens of private offices. The government is planning to open two more clinics as well to treat children, pregnant women, and the elderly. In 1985, the government spent 6.8 percent of its budget on health-related matters.

Macao has a long history of caring for the poor and needy. The Santa Casa de Misericordia, founded by Portugal's Queen Leonor in 1498 to care for orphans, still operates after more than 400 years. The nuns who run the orphanage also operate a hospital and a leper colony on Coloane Island. Another old charitable institution is the

Hospital of the Poor, founded in the early 1600s. It cares for destitute Macaons without regard to their race or color.

Transportation

Macao is not easy to get to. There are only two ways to get there: by boat or via a narrow paved road that runs to Macao from the Chinese city of Canton, 70 miles (113 kilometers) to the north. But crossing the border from China requires numerous permits. Therefore, the more than four million visitors who arrive in Macao each year usually come on a ferry boat from Hong Kong.

Until a few years ago, the Hong Kong ferry was extremely slow, taking about three hours for the 40-mile (64-kilometer) trip. This slow ferry still operates, and many travelers enjoy its lounges and private cabins. But those who want to make the trip in less time can now take more modern boats, such as jetfoils, jetcats, hydrofoils, and high-speed ferries.

The jetfoils are the fastest method of water transportation, skimming across the water from Hong Kong to Macao in just 55 minutes. The larger jetcats (jet-propelled ferries that can carry up to 215 passengers) are the next fastest, making the trip in 70 minutes. Hydrofoils take 75 minutes, and high-speed ferries, which carry as many as 690 people, can make the crossing in about 100 minutes.

To handle this faster traffic, Hong Kong has built a new ferry terminal. The $250 million Shun Tak terminal is one of the most advanced marine terminals in the world, handling up to 90,000 passengers daily. Macao began to build its own new terminal in January 1987. It should be finished in time for the Chinese New Year, 1988, when thousands of tourists will flood Macao.

For years, Macao has considered constructing an airport, but the project has never advanced beyond the planning stages. (Tentative plans call for the airport to be built on reclaimed land between the islands of Coloane and Taipa.) Similarly, the government has

Many tourists travel in jetfoils, which can reach Hong Kong in less than an hour.

long discussed the possibility of building a deep-water port for shipping. Macao's shipping ports face serious problems because the silt carried in from the Pearl River often blocks both the Inner and Outer harbors. A deep-water harbor would solve this problem, but so far no plans have been approved.

Another transportation project that has been planned but not executed is the construction of a railroad between Macao and the nearby Special Economic Zone of Zhuhai in China. (Special economic zones are cities built by China to increase industrial production.) The $2-billion railroad, to be funded by the Chinese government, would link Macao with both Zhuhai and Canton.

Although it may be difficult to reach, Macao is easy to get around in. Visitors can use bikes, cars, or buses to move from place to place. The most common form of transportation in Macao is the automobile. More than 17,000 cars, most of them Japanese-made, clog the territory's 56 miles (90 kilometers) of roadway. Macao also has an extensive bus system that travels throughout the city and to both of the islands.

Another popular mode of transportation is the bicycle. Thousands of Macaons ride bikes to and from work or school. But perhaps the most enjoyable way to travel around Macao is in a pedicab, a large tricycle that seats two. Macao is one of the few places in Asia that still uses pedicabs. They are inexpensive to rent. A short trip costs just a few cents, and a pedicab can be hired for the equivalent of about U.S. $3 to $4 per hour. But riders must bargain with the cab owner to determine the fare before the ride begins.

The Media

Macao has sophisticated news media. Nine daily newspapers are published in the territory, three in Portuguese (one is the government's official paper) and six in Chinese. Surveys show that more than half the city's adult population reads one of these papers.

Several magazines are also available, including *Sisters Pictorial*, *Reader's Digest Chinese*, *Ladies and Home*, and *Mign Pao Monthly*. These magazines are read mostly by Macao's well-educated single young women.

Those who would rather watch than read can tune into Macao's government-owned television station, Teledifusão de Macao (TDM). It broadcasts 35 hours of programming each week, including news, entertainment, and live coverage of such things as Macao's annual Grand Prix race. Shows are broadcast in both Chinese and Portuguese. TDM faces competition from private stations beamed in from Hong Kong, which offer a wide variety of Chinese and English programs. Despite the variety of programming, however, only 1 in 450 Macaons owns a television set.

Drivers now pedal rickshaws, or pedicabs. They used to pull them on foot.

TDM also runs two radio channels, one broadcast in Portuguese, the other in Chinese. A private radio station offers Chinese programs, and the government recently built a new satellite ground station to improve international telecommunications. Radio is much more popular than television—one in every six people in Macao owns a radio.

Gambling has been Macao's number-one source of income ever since it was legalized in 1844. This picture shows a gambling house at the turn of the century.

Revitalizing a Trade Economy

Unlike most countries, Macao has absolutely no natural resources. No forests, oil reserves, coal mines, or veins of gold can be found in the territory. Yet, despite strong competition from other Asian countries, Macao's economy has grown steadily in recent years. It has moved from the trade economy of centuries past to a modern economy based on gambling, manufacturing, and tourism.

Legalized gambling is Macao's primary source of income. The territory has five casinos, all licensed and controlled by the government. The casinos are under contract with the government-licensed gambling syndicate known as Sociedade de Turismo e Diversoes de Macao (the Macao Tourism and Entertainment Society). The contract requires the society to pay Macao's government a gambling tax amounting to 26 percent of its annual gambling earnings or $45 million, whichever sum is larger. This tax provides the government with more than 40 percent of its annual income.

Each year, millions of visitors pour into the tiny territory to take their chances at the gaming tables. In 1985, 4.3 million people—an average of 11,781 per day—visited Macao and spent more than $256 million. More than 80 percent of these visitors came from Hong Kong. Most of the rest came from Japan.

In the past, most of Macao's visitors came to the territory for one day only—they gambled, toured the islands, and then returned to Hong Kong or Japan. Recently, Macao has tried to encourage these visitors to stay longer, and thus to spend more money on hotel rooms, food, and souvenirs. The territory hopes to attract more international travelers by offering trips across the border into China.

Industrial Development

In the past 20 years, manufacturing centers have sprung up throughout Macao. Today, raw goods, such as cloth and wood, are made into clothing and furniture in the territory's industrial areas, then exported for sale abroad. Macao has built a strong economy in this fashion. It has a favorable trade balance, which means that it exports more than it imports (therefore earning more than its spends). The government uses its trade surplus to pay for various projects, including street repair and removing silt from the harbor.

Macao's prosperity is relatively recent. Until the mid-1960s, the territory was underdeveloped and depended on the gambling casinos and an illegal gold trade for its livelihood. It earned most of its revenue by legally importing gold and then smuggling it into areas, such as Hong Kong, that prohibited gold trading. The government turned a blind eye to this practice because it received a lot of tax money from the gold imports. But since the late 1960s, new economic opportunities have lessened the need for the illegal trade. Attracted by inexpensive land and labor, industrial developers from Hong Kong have set up their factories in Macao, creating a profitable manufacturing center.

Macao continues to diversify its manufacturing industries. Today, it sells clothing, toys, furniture, artificial flowers, optical and photographic equipment, porcelain, and electronics. Macao's clothing firms were originally small shops where dozens of women labored to cut and sew garments. Although such shops still exist, modern,

These women work in a textile factory. The territory exports both fabric and finished garments.

computerized factories are replacing them. One of the largest clothing factories in Macao can produce some 3,000 different designs at the same time. This and other new factories have brought about a steady increase in export sales. In 1985, garment sales accounted for 69 percent of Macao's export earnings.

After clothing, Macao's most important export is toys. They account for more than 11 percent of export sales. Although toy manufacturing is a relatively new development, it has become a fast-growing industry, thanks in part to investors from Hong Kong and China. Today, Macao's toys range from die-cast metal cars to electronic robots.

Macao's busy port teems with activity throughout the year.

Another of Macao's small but growing industries is furniture design and construction, which grew out of the traditional Chinese art of wood carving. Furniture in both Chinese and Western styles ranges from tables and chairs to desks and fine cabinets. Some pieces are intricately carved and then inlaid with tiny pieces of mother-of-pearl in Chinese designs.

Another industry is making imitation flowers from silk or from such man-made products as plastic and nylon. Porcelain, an ancient Chinese product, is a major export. Factories import unglazed pots and vases from China, then paint and glaze them in Macao for shipment to markets around the world. Two other fields, opticals and electronics, are also growing rapidly. Optical products include cameras and binoculars, and Macao's electronics factories turn out portable radios, clock-radios, and cassette recorders.

In recent years, Macao has attracted more international banks to its shores. Banks from England, the United States, France, Hong Kong, and Shanghai have set up shop in the tiny territory. These banks provide the Macaons with a large source of credit money that they can use to establish new businesses. Government figures show that credit to individuals and companies jumped 24 percent in 1985, to $1 billion. Nearly one-third of this credit funded new construction and public works projects, indicating Macao's continued growth.

Macao intends to continue its industrial development. Dr. Carlos Monjardino, secretary for the economy, has reported that the government is encouraging production of food products, pharmaceuticals, car batteries, musical instruments, silk fabrics, and more clothing. Dr. Monjardino believes that these industries will be ideal for Macao because they do not require a great deal of space or produce pollution.

The Standard of Living

About 60 percent of Macao's adults, including half of all women, work for a living. Those who do not work include housewives (about 22 percent of the adult population), students (9 percent), and the retired (also about 9 percent). Of the working population, 46 percent are employed in factories or shops, 9 percent work in offices, 4 percent are traders or shop owners, and 1 percent work as executives.

The average unskilled worker in Macao makes about 32 patacás (the equivalent of about U.S. $4) for a full day's work. Pay of $4 a day—less than many earn per hour in the Unites States—means that the average person earns little more than $1,000 per year. Although the costs of food, clothing, and housing are much less than in the United States, most of these workers do not live well. Many can find housing only in squatter shacks on the edge of the city or on one of the islands. Although workers with more skills and higher education earn much more, most wealthy people in Macao are Chinese

Macaons on Coloane Island live in traditional Chinese houses in rural villages.

or European businesspeople. The average Macaon must watch his patacás carefully.

Chinese Influence

In recent years, China has steadily taken a larger role in Macao's economy. In 1985, China sold more than $182 million worth of goods to Macao, and it now has six banks and many commercial and financial representatives in the tiny territory. The largest of these firms is the Nam Kwong Company, which handles most of China's import and export trade with Macao.

China's increased role in Macao has raised questions about the territory's economic future. The Macaon people are concerned about China's Communist economic system, which does not allow individuals to own businesses (in the Communist system, the government controls all factories, farms, and shops). Macao is a capitalist territory, in which individuals run private businesses for personal profit. Although some Macaons have expressed fears that China might try to alter Macao's economy, it is unlikely. China has changed its outlook on economic development in recent years, and its shift toward free enterprise is expected to continue.

Macaon officials now believe that when Macao returns to Chinese authority, China will become one country with two economic systems. Macao will be part of China, but it will still continue to have a capitalist, rather than a Communist, economy. Macao's long history as a trade center for southern China is expected to continue.

A cluster of modern skyscrapers along the harbor shows how Macao has grown. In 1513, when Jorge Álvares landed here, the only buildings were a few fishermen's shacks.

A Last Look at Macao

Over the past four centuries, the tiny territory of Macao has proven its ability to adapt to the times. Although it lacks natural resources and deep harbors, Macao managed to build a profitable trade economy. After its trading monopoly collapsed, it succeeded in developing other industries to ensure its livelihood. And although great cultural differences exist between its Portuguese government and its Chinese population, it has created a colorful society that respects both European and Oriental ways of life.

When Portuguese explorer Jorge Álvares first sighted Macao in 1513, it was nothing more than a rocky little peninsula dotted with a few fishermen's shacks. But as Portuguese trade in the region expanded, Macao quickly became an important link between Europe and China. After the Chinese government permitted the Portuguese to establish a community in 1557, Macao became the hub of Asian trade. It secured a monopoly on trade between China and Japan, and Portuguese profiteers sold Chinese silk for Japanese silver. The colony thrived.

In addition to being a rich trading center, Macao became the base for Catholic missionary work in Asia. Catholic monks built great churches on the rocky peninsula, and Japanese Christians poured into Macao to escape persecution in their own country. Macao became a European metropolis in the middle of Asia.

Macao's privileged position soon attracted envious competition, however. Dutch and British traders—and pirates from a variety of nations—attacked the colony and sacked its ships. Macao was able to repel many of these assaults, but the golden era of Portuguese trade in Asia could not last forever. In 1641, the Dutch captured the Portuguese colony of Malacca in Malaya. At about the same time, the rich trade with Japan ended after Japanese rulers, fearing the growing Christian influence, closed their doors to all outsiders. Macao was virtually cut off from the rest of the world.

In the early 1700s, more countries began trading with China, using Macao as the center for operations. For a brief time, the territory enjoyed a sound economy. But this period of prosperity ended in 1841, when the British captured Hong Kong. With its natural deep-water harbor, Hong Kong swiftly replaced Macao as the center for trade with southern China.

By 1900, the once-busy harbor held only a handful of Chinese sailing junks and small sampans.

In the century that followed, Macao was reduced to a sleepy Asian outpost, a reminder of glories past. People came to gamble in Macao's casinos, but few took the tiny territory seriously. Today, however, it thrives. Macao City, the most densely populated place on earth, bustles with activity. Tourists crowd its gambling casinos and resort hotels, international bankers fill its high-rise office buildings, and workers its manufacturing plants. The government is now building new roads, schools, and health-care facilities, and is planning a larger harbor and an airport.

Macao faces many problems. Many of its workers live in poverty in squatter shacks on the city's edge or on fishing junks that crowd the Pearl River. The tiny territory has run out of space for housing or industrial development. While the government attempts to resolve these problems, it must also face the impending change in Macao's status from a Portuguese territory to part of Communist China.

The prospect of Macao's return to China worries many Macaons. They fear that the change in government will destroy Macao's industrial economy and endanger the freedom of its Chinese refugees. The Chinese government has promised that life in Macao will not be dramatically altered when China assumes control. But only time will tell what Chinese rule will bring.

As tiny Macao prepares to return to Chinese control, an era that began nearly 450 years ago with Portugal's age of exploration is about to end. But the people of Macao have adapted to many changes in the past four centuries, and they have always adjusted and prospered. The future seems unlikely to alter that.

GLOSSARY

A-Ma The Chinese goddess who protects fishermen. Macao takes its name from a temple dedicated to her.

Barrier Gate A gate erected by the Chinese on the China-Macao border to prevent Portuguese settlers from entering mainland China.

Boxer Rebellion An uprising against foreigners that occurred in China in 1900, sending a wave of immigrants into Macao.

Buddhism The religion practiced by most Chinese in Macao. It is based on the teachings of Siddhartha Gautama, a 5th century B.C. leader known as the Buddha.

Ch'un tze A mixture of sticky rice, port, lotus seeds, and boiled egg yolks wrapped in bamboo leaves. It is eaten during the annual Dragon Boat Festival.

Colonialism A system in which one power controls and sometimes exploits a dependent area or people.

Communism A system of government in which the state owns all businesses and allocates resources to individuals on the basis of need.

Confucius A 5th-century B.C. philosopher whose teachings are followed by many of Macao's Chinese inhabitants.

Cultural Revolution A mass campaign, undertaken by Chinese leader Mao Tse-Tung from 1966 to 1969, that attempted to rid China of old ideas, customs, culture, and habits by attacking people who disagreed with the new Communist state.

Dai sui A betting game in which players guess which numbers will come up after three dice are thrown. Literally translated, the name means "big and small."

Delta A land deposit (or a series of deposits) at the mouth of a river.

Fan-tan A Chinese game in which players bet on the number of white beads that will remain in a silver cup after the dealer divides the cup's contents by four.

Feijoadas A Brazilian stew made of pork, spicy sausage, beans, cabbage, and potatoes. The Portuguese introduced it to Macao, where it has become a popular dish.

Jetfoil A high-speed water craft used to transport people from Hong Kong to Macao in less than 55 minutes.

Joss stick A piece of incense burned inside a Chinese temple in front of a joss, or idol.

Junk A Chinese sailing ship.

Kabaya A type of robe, originally worn in Malaysia, that many Macaon women used to wear.

Kain A type of Malayan blouse, formerly worn by many Macaon women.

Leal Senado The Loyal Senate, once Macao's most important governing body. Today, it handles municipal matters.

Mooncakes Sugary, golden-colored buns that are filled with bean paste, lotus seeds, or pork and eaten during the Mooncake Festival.

Opium War	A war that erupted between Great Britain and China when the Chinese tried to stop the British trade in opium, a narcotic extracted from poppies. It lasted from 1839 until 1842.
Pedicab	A large, two-seater tricycle used as a common form of transportation in Macao. A pedicab can be hired for only U.S. $3 to $4 per hour.
Peninsula	A body of land connected to a larger land mass and almost completely surrounded by water.
Skekwan	A type of statuary that is produced near the Chinese city of Canton and exhibited in Macao's Camões Museum.
Spice Islands	A name given to Indonesia during the 15th and 16th centuries, when Europeans traded in its spices.
Taoism	A philosophy that is commonly practiced in conjunction with Macaon Buddhism. Based on the teachings of the ancient Chinese philosopher Lao-tzu, it stresses that all natural things have opposites of equal strength.
Tsao Wang	The kitchen god who is believed to travel to heaven on the eve of the Chinese New Year to report a family's activities to the gods.
Typhoon	A tropical storm common to the islands off the Chinese coast. It takes its name from the Chinese words *ta-fung*, meaning "great wind."
yang	The word the Chinese use to describe the masculine part of the year, during which the days are long and hot.
Yang kuei	A Chinese term meaning "foreign devils." During the 1500s, it was used to describe the Portuguese settlers in Macao.
yin	The Chinese word for the feminine part of the year, when the days are dark and cool.

PICTURE CREDITS

Bettmann Archive (pp. 29, 31, 39, 76); Macao Tourist Information Bureau (cover; pp. 2, 14, 20, 24, 26, 27, 33, 36, 41, 42–43 (below), 44 (above), 45, 46 (below), 46–47, 48, 52, 58, 60, 63, 66, 69, 70, 72, 78, 80, 86); Keith W. Strandberg (pp. 42 (above), 43, 44 (below), 46 (above), 47, 48 (above), 56, 62, 74, 82, 84); UPI/Bettmann Newsphotos (pp. 16–17, 35, 50).

INDEX

A
acupuncture 69
Advisory Council 67
Africa 26, 39
airport, plans for 71
Alvares, Jorge 27, 85
A-Ma, goddess and temple 25, 40, 64
Amacão, Amagão 26
ancestor veneration 40
annual income 81
architecture 60–65
art 54, 55
Asia 15, 86
astrologers 53

B
banking 81, 82, 87
Barrier Gate 27
Boxer Rebellion 17, 33
Brazil 38
breakwater 22
Buddha, Gautama 40, 63, 64
Buddhism 40
Buddhist temples 18, 39
burial customs 53

C
Camões, Luis Vaz de 55
Canton 15, 21, 27, 30, 31, 55, 71, 73
Cantonese language 38

capitalism 15
casinos 16, 57, 77, 87
cathedrals 28, 40, 60, 61
Catholicism 40
Catholic missionaries 15, 16, 28, 29, 85
China 15, 18, 19, 21, 25, 26, 27, 28, 30, 31, 32, 33, 34, 35, 49, 55, 64, 67, 78, 79, 80, 82, 85, 87
Christ, Jesus 61
Chu Chaing-k'ou (Pearl River) 21
ch'un tze 49
Ch'u Yuan 49
churches 15, 18, 28
Churchill, Lord John Spenser 65
Churchill, Sir Winston 65
Citadel of São Paulo 61
climate 23
Coloane 21, 22, 23, 65, 70, 71
communism 15, 82
communist system 83
Confucius 40
Cross of Jerusalem 61
cuisine 38
Cushing, Caleb 64

D
dai sui 56
debts, payment of 51
doctors 68
Dragon Boat Festival 49

◀93▶

dress styles 38
drinking water supply 22
Dutch raids 29, 30, 52, 61, 80

E
East Indies, 15
economy 16, 18, 31, 35, 77–83
education 18, 68
English language 38, 68
Enlightened One (Buddha) 40, 64
European influence 15, 18, 38, 54, 55
exports 35, 78, 79, 80

F
factories 27, 79
fan-tan 57
ferry services 71
festivals 49–52
Fifth Moon Festival 49
fishermen 15, 22, 25, 37
food crops 38
forts 61
fortune tellers 53, 64
France 81
free enterprise 83
Fukian province 25
funerals 53

G
gambling 16, 17, 31, 56–57, 77, 87
gold trade, illegal 78
government, system of 67
governor 67
Goa 38
Great Britain 16, 25, 30, 81
Guia fort 61

H
harbor 15, 18, 25, 72, 86

health care, 18, 68–70
herbal medicine 69
Historical Archives 56
holidays 18, 49–52
Holy Spirit 61
Hong Kong 18, 31, 32, 35, 71, 74, 77, 78, 79, 81, 86
horse racing (trotters) 65
hospitals 70
hotels 65
housing 18, 22, 23, 28, 37, 59, 81, 87
Hsian Shan island 21
"hungry tigers" 57

I
imports 80, 82
India 26, 30, 38
Indonesia 15, 26
industry 17, 78, 79, 80, 87

J
Japan 15, 26, 27, 28, 29, 30, 77, 78, 85, 86
    Macao mission to 30
Japanese Christians 29, 30, 60

K
kabayas 38
kains 38
Ki Ying 64
Kuan Yin 25, 40, 41, 49, 64
Kuan Yin temple 25, 62–64
    site of Sino-U.S. treaty 64
Kum Iam 62

L
Ladrones Islands 21
landfill projects 22
Lantau 21

Lao-tzu, philosopher 40
Lappa 22
Leal Senado 61, 67
Legislative Assembly 67
leper colony 70
lighthouse 61
Lin Fong temple 49
lion dance 51
literacy 68
literature 55
lunar calendar 50–51
Lusiadas 55

M
Macanese 37
Macao
    change of status 18, 19, 35, 87
    motto 62
    site of U.S.-China treaty 64
Macao City 22, 87
Macao Tourism Society 77
magazines 73
Malacca 26, 28, 30, 86
Malaya 86
Manchu dynasty 55, 56
manufacturing 19, 77, 78, 79
Marco Polo 64
marriage customs 53
medical clinics 70
midwives 69
Military Museum 56
Ming Dynasty 63
Monte Forte fortress 61
Mooncake Festival 49
mourners, professional 53
Municipal Council 67

N
Nagasaki Christian uprising 29

National Library 56
National People's Congress 67
natural resources 77
Netherlands 16, 25, 29
news media 73–75
nurses 69

O
opera, Chinese 51
opium smuggling 30
Opium War 30
orphan care 70

P
Pearl River 15, 21, 22, 25, 72, 87
pedicabs 73
Philippine Islands 28
Pinto, Fernão Mendes 27
pirates 21, 27, 86
population 17, 22, 33, 37, 87
ports 22, 72
Portugal 15, 16, 18, 25, 28, 29, 31, 35, 38, 67, 68
    gets right to build 27
    offers to return Macao 35
    revolution in 35
    seeks trading agreement 27, 31, 87
    treaty talks 32–33
Portuguese capture fort 32
    defeat pirates 27
    discover Macao 27
    land in Japan 27
Portuguese explorers 26, 27, 38, 39, 85
    governor assassinated 32
    heritage 18, 60
    language 38, 73, 74, 75
    National Assembly 67

traders 15, 26–31, 38
wines 39
public works 81

R
radio stations 75
railroad, plans for 73
rainfall 23
raw goods 78
refugees 17, 18, 33, 87
religious worship 39, 40, 49–52
revenue 77
riots 34, 35

S
St. Paul's Cathedral 28, 60–61
Santa Casa de Misericordia 70
schools 68
seasons 23, 50
Shanghai 81
shipbuilding 28
shogun 29, 30
silk trade 15, 26, 27, 28, 85
silver 15, 27, 28, 85
social services 70–71
South China Sea 21, 22
Spain 16, 25, 28, 29
Special Economic Zones 73
Spice Islands 26
spice trade 15, 26, 28
standard of living 18, 81–82
street layout 59
street vendors 59
Sun Yat-sen 55–56

T
ta-fung 23
Taipa island 21, 22, 23, 65, 71
Tao 40
Tao Te Ching 40

temples 25, 40, 49, 51, 59, 62, 64, 65
Thailand 26
topography 21, 22
tourism 17, 21, 71, 77, 78
trade 15, 16, 19, 25–35, 82, 85, 86
trade surplus 18, 78
transportation 71–73
treaty ceding Macao to Portuguese 32–33
treaty of friendship, Sino-U.S. 64
Treaty of Nanking 30
Tsao Wang, kitchen god 51
typhoon 23

U
United States 64, 81
University of East Asia 65, 68
unskilled workers 81

V
Vasco da Gama 26
vegetation 21
Virgin Mary 61
visitors 71–77
voting rights 68

W
wages 18, 81
wealth distribution 81, 82
work force 81
Wu Yueh Chieh festival 49

Y
yang 50
yin 50
yang kuei 27

Z
Zhuhai, 73